ESSENTIAL LIFESKILLS

Th
Under

D0625553

Philippa Davies

LONDON, NEW YORK, MUNICH,
MELBOURNE, DELHI

Project Editor Nicky Munro
Senior Art Editor Sarah Cowley
DTP Designer Rajen Shah
Production Controller Mandy Inness

Managing Editor Adèle Hayward
Managing Art Editor Marianne Markham
Category Publisher Stephanie Jackson

Produced for Dorling Kindersley by
Cooling Brown
9–11 High Street, Hampton
Middlesex TW12 2SA.

Creative Director Arthur Brown
Managing Editor Amanda Lebentz
Designer Elaine Hewson
Editors Alex Edmonds, Alison Bolus

First published in Great Britain in 2003
by Dorling Kindersley Limited, 80 Strand
London WC2R 0RL.

A Penguin Company

2 4 6 8 10 9 7 5 3

A CIP catalogue record for this book is available
from the British Library.
ISBN 0 7513 4896 1

Reproduced by Colourscan, Singapore
Printed in Hong Kong by Wing King Tong

See our complete catalogue at
www.dk.com

Contents

Introduction

Everyone feels pressure at some time in life, and when viewed as a challenge and handled well, it can prove highly stimulating and inspiring. Only when pressure becomes overwhelming does it result in exhaustion, ill health, or unhappiness. Thriving Under Pressure will help you understand what causes pressure, how it can benefit you, and how it can lead to stress. The book provides practical advice on preparing yourself mentally and physically to do your best under pressure and avoid anxiety, even when facing major life changes, such as moving home, suffering a bereavement, or adapting to parenthood. Packed with inspirational quotations, useful exercises, tips, and questionnaires, this invaluable book will ensure that you do not just survive under pressure – but that you are truly able to thrive on it.

Understanding Pressure

Pressure can bring out the best in people, provided it is managed well. Learn what causes pressure and how to recognize the point at which you cease to thrive and start to feel stressed.

Defining Pressure

*P*ressure can be a motivating force. It is felt when there is a sense of urgency or when demands are being made of you. Learn what constitutes pressure and how you are likely to respond to it to assess whether you need to manage it more effectively.

WHAT IS PRESSURE?

Pressure takes many forms. It may be generated by other people, or situations, or it may be self-imposed. Pressure can occur when you are working to deadlines, having to perform several different roles – such as parent, partner, son or daughter, and boss – at the same time, or having to cope with setbacks or change. Major changes, such as moving home or suffering a bereavement, inevitably bring a high level of pressure because they involve anxiety and uncertainty. Pressure is also cumulative, so experiencing a series of minor incidents can cause pressure to rise significantly.

▲ **Taking a break**
If you are to thrive at work, it is important to take proper lunch breaks. Getting away from your desk, even if only for a short period, will give you more energy and focus for the afternoon.

RESPONDING TO PRESSURE

Everyone responds to pressure differently. What is a challenge to one individual might be an immense pressure to another. Your own response to pressure will often be determined by your lifestyle, social and professional involvements, age, culture, gender, education, and genetic factors. Your state of mind and physical health at the time will also have an influence on the level of pressure that you feel.

▼ **Understanding reactions to pressure**
When pressure is well-managed, it can spur you on to greater achievement, whereas an inability to handle pressure can result in adverse reactions, including increased vulnerability to stress.

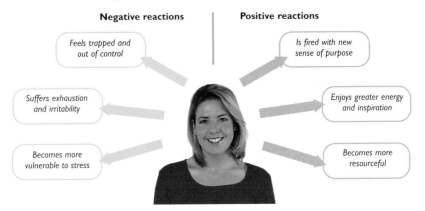

Negative reactions

Feels trapped and out of control

Suffers exhaustion and irritability

Becomes more vulnerable to stress

Positive reactions

Is fired with new sense of purpose

Enjoys greater energy and inspiration

Becomes more resourceful

Understanding Levels of Pressure

Level of Pressure	Examples
Minor	Short-term irritants, such as sitting next to a heavy smoker in a wine bar, or someone listening to loud music on the train.
Medium	Demanding situations, such as attending a job interview, having to make a speech, or handling a conflict at work.
High	Extremely demanding events, such as the death of someone close, experiencing serious illness, or redundancy.

Analyzing the Positive Aspects of Pressure

Pressure is known to stimulate the body and mind, producing a variety of advantageous effects. Recognize how pressure can maximize your performance and creativity, increase confidence, and promote a general sense of well-being.

INSPIRING ACHIEVEMENT

The knowledge that there is a set time frame in which to achieve a goal can be highly motivational. When you have limited time, you are more likely to give a task your full attention, sustaining concentration for longer periods and prioritizing your activities in the most effective way. When you are absorbed in a project and experiencing total commitment to what you are doing, you tend to enjoy it more. Your performance is likely to improve, too, because a degree of pressure can help you feel more energetic and able to keep going for longer periods. Provided that pressure is kept at manageable levels, it can motivate you to produce high-quality work, reliably, over a long period.

Finding creative solutions ▶
Working with other people to meet an impending deadline often encourages you to move away from set patterns of thinking and generate creative solutions.

Expectant mother explains that room must be decorated before baby is born

Designer looks at ways of altering scheme to save time

8

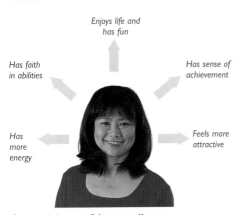

Enjoys life and
has fun

Has faith
in abilities

Has sense of
achievement

Has
more
energy

Feels more
attractive

▲ **Acquiring confident attributes**
*Being under pressure can help people realize just how resourceful
they can be. The more experience of thriving under pressure you
have, the more confident and authoritative you will become.*

BUILDING CONFIDENCE

Experiencing pressure and handling it well encourages you to acknowledge your strengths and therefore increases your self-esteem. Each time you experience a similar challenge, you will become more confident in your ability to cope. After a period of pressure, reflect on how well you managed and give yourself praise. Remember the sense of achievement you feel, and recall it to keep your confidence high when pressure looms in the future.

ENHANCING WELL-BEING

Because pressure acts like a stimulant, it heightens the senses and makes you more alert to what is happening around you. As a result, you may take more pleasure in eating good food, enjoy exercise more, and appreciate more fully the good things in your life. You may also find that you sleep better, that your sex life improves, and that relationships with friends and family are more harmonious. However, in rising to the challenge of pressure, it is important to avoid overdoing it. Everyone needs a break from pressure, so give yourself time off regularly.

Feeling strong ▶
*Regular exercise boosts energy, giving you
increased stamina. The fitter and stronger
you are, the better you handle pressure.*

> ## FOCUS POINT
>
> ● Build up your fitness gradually if it has been some time since you exercised regularly.

Is able to perform more
sit-ups with less effort

Looking at the Causes of Pressure

Work, relationships, major life events, and simply handling everyday situations can all create problems. Identify your primary sources of pressure and monitor these areas of your life to prevent anxiety from rising to stressful levels.

66When work is a pleasure, life is a joy! When work is a duty, life is slavery.99

Maxim Gorky

RECOGNIZING WORK STRESSES

Developments in communications technology, increased competition, and the demise of jobs for life mean that today's work climate is volatile and unpredictable. As workloads increase and staff are put under more pressure to be productive, many people find that they are working longer hours in order to meet tight deadlines or high targets. Many people also have to deal with a daily barrage of e-mails in addition to telephone calls, faxes, and face-to-face meetings, leaving little time to advance work projects. Other forms of pressure include being overqualified, unclear about a job description, or fearful of making mistakes.

Learns new software programme

◀ **Updating skills**
Keep abreast of advances in technology in your field of work, and update your skills to avoid the stress of feeling "left behind" in the workplace.

▼ Sharing responsibility
The pressures of family life are greatly reduced when every member makes a valid contribution and there is a spirit of sharing and cooperation.

FULFILLING SEVERAL ROLES

A common cause of pressure is attempting to fulfil several different roles at once. Catering to other people's demands while trying to organize your own life can make you feel stretched in every direction. Someone suffering from role overload may be caring for elderly relatives, looking after children, running a home, and even pursuing a career. Friends can also add to the pressure by making too many demands on you. If you feel overloaded, discuss the problem with those close to you. If you suppress your emotions you risk feeling stressed and resentful.

EXAMINING LIFE PRESSURES

While the pressures of modern life are many, experiencing a number of difficult life events in a short period of time increases the amount of pressure you are likely to feel. Financial worries alone may cause you concern, but when combined with illness or injury and disagreements with relatives, friends, or neighbours, the level of worry rises considerably. The better you understand the effect such events are likely to have on you, the more easily you will be able to prepare yourself in advance for similar events in the future.

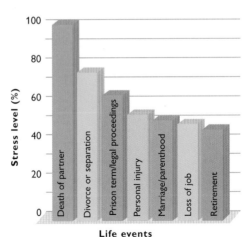

Stress level (%)

Life events: Death of partner, Divorce or separation, Prison term/legal proceedings, Personal injury, Marriage/parenthood, Loss of job, Retirement

Life events

▲ **Identifying the most stressful life events**
Research has revealed that the death of a partner tops the list of life's most stressful events. Even positive events, such as becoming a parent, can cause tremendous stress.

Understanding How Pressure Leads to Stress

When pressure builds to such a high level that it becomes difficult to handle, it can lead to harmful stress. Improve your understanding of stress by learning how the body reacts to it, and how it can affect your behaviour.

UNDERSTANDING STRESS

Stress is a universal reaction experienced by both humans and animals. It occurs when events challenge people's abilities to respond to them. Austrian researcher Dr Hans Selye, who became known as the "father of stress" for his pioneering work into the condition during the 1930s, described stress as the body's "non-specific response to any demand – pleasant or not". Today, it is known that an individual's characteristics, and the context in which stress occurs, also affect his or her ability to cope. Stress often invokes anxiety and provokes both physical and pyschological reactions – indeed, these are inextricably linked.

Offers to help friend, who looks tired and overstretched

Realizes that she has been doing too much

Preventing stress ▶
If friends or family comment that you are doing too much, listen to them. You may need their help if you are to prevent pressure from turning to stress.

REACTING PHYSICALLY

When you find yourself in a pressured situation, a series of biochemical and physiological events occurs in your body to prepare you for action. Often called the "fight or flight" response, this reaction is temporary and the body returns to a stable state once the perceived danger has passed. However, when pressure builds or continues over a period, the body reacts as if under constant stress, producing chemicals that depress the immune system.

Fact File

In acutely stressful situations, blood flow is diverted away from the skin to support the heart and muscle tissues. The physical effect is a cool, clammy, sweaty skin and a tightening of the scalp so that the hair seems to stand on end.

Hypothalamus triggers release of adrenaline and cortisol into bloodstream

Blood supply is directed to muscles

Breathing becomes rapid

Heart rate increases

Adrenal glands produce more adrenaline

Recognizing the body's response to stress ▶
The physical symptoms of stress can affect the whole body, particularly the cardiac and respiratory systems. If experienced continuously over a long period of time, they can seriously damage health.

Self-Talk

Use the following affirmations to help you avoid resorting to short-term coping mechanisms when under pressure.

❝I am strong enough to survive on my own.❞

❝Smoking, drinking, or taking drugs will not solve any problems.❞

❝When I am feeling stressed, I know I can take positive action to alleviate it.❞

CHANGING NORMAL PATTERNS OF BEHAVIOUR

When pressure turns to stress, many people change their behaviour in order to cope. They may start to spend more time alone because they feel exhausted or depressed. Alternatively, they might seek out company and want to socialize almost every night as a way of escaping their problems. If people tell you that you have changed, or you find yourself behaving out of character, ask yourself why. If your concentration or memory are poor, you are short-tempered, irritable, over-emotional, apathetic, or sad, be aware that these are all common indications of stress and need to be addressed.

Recognizing Stress

Everyone reacts differently to stress and some people are able to handle it more easily than others. Consider whether you are experiencing any of the common emotional or physical symptoms to assess whether you need to manage stress more effectively.

Notes emotions after a hectic day

▲ **Recording your feelings**
Keep a diary of how you are feeling during pressurized periods, so that you can monitor your moods and be aware when the signs point to harmful stress.

READING EMOTIONAL SIGNS

The emotional symptoms of extreme stress include panic or anxiety attacks, phobias, depression, anger, eating disorders, and low self-esteem. Erratic behaviour, mood swings, depression, loss of sense of humour, and an inability to make decisions are all common signs. You should also be concerned if you lose interest in your personal appearance, other people, or activities that you previously enjoyed. Changes in behaviour may also strain relationships with friends and family. If you notice symptoms of stress, try to ease up for a short period, get more sleep, adopt stress management techniques, or alter your lifestyle so that you become more stress-resistant.

FINDING SHORT-TERM RELIEF

As a temporary relief from stress, many people turn to "false friends". Cigarettes, far from calming you down, contain nicotine, which is a stimulant, and long-term effects include cancer, heart disease, and respiratory illness. Caffeine is another stimulant that activates the adrenal glands and contributes to the negative effects of stress over time. Alcohol may feel relaxing in the short-term but long-term, it reduces the body's ability to withstand stress.

Avoiding "false friends"
Sugar, alcohol, caffeine, and nicotine are unhealthy "mood enhancers" that can contribute to stress if used to excess.

SPOTTING PHYSICAL SYMPTOMS

Certain physical symptoms of stress, such as high blood pressure and heart disease, can be life-threatening. Less serious physical signs include insomnia, ulcers, headaches, and digestive disorders, such as irritable bowel syndrome. Sleep disturbances, feelings of constant fatigue, and a worsening of skin disorders, such as eczema and acne, are also common symptoms. Extreme stress may also lead to diminished sex drive and even impotence. All these symptoms, of course, may be caused by factors other than stress, and any recurring or serious health problems should always be checked out by a doctor.

Recurrent headaches

Puffy, bloodshot eyes

Pain resulting from muscle tension

Tightness in chest

▲ **Feeling the physical effects of stress**
Stress is known to cause tension headaches, which sometimes do not start until long after a stressful event is over. Tension can also lead to nagging aches and pains.

Case Study

NAME: Chris
ISSUE: Pushes himself too hard
OBJECTIVE: To relax and enjoy life

Chris is the managing director of a large commercial company. Achievement is extremely important to him and gives him a sense of self-worth. Chris works at a very fast pace and feels impatient with colleagues who work more slowly. People are always telling him that he does too much, and he has little time to relax. Chris begins to experience severe stomach pains, and is diagnosed with a peptic ulcer. On his doctor's orders, Chris takes an extended holiday. For the first time in years, he completely relaxes, and decides that he would like to continue feeling this way. On his return, Chris shifts his focus and energy towards his relationships and looks for more creative, relaxing pastimes to help build his self-worth. He ruthlessly prunes his schedule so that he has gaps in his diary. Chris now takes pressure in his stride and has found contentment in life.

Increasing Stress Resistance

There are certain people who seem to be particularly well-equipped to deal with pressure. Follow the example of these "hardy individuals", as psychologists call them, who have achieved a balance in life, focus on the present, and have a strong sense of purpose.

Breathes gently from the diaphragm

LEADING A BALANCED LIFE

In order to resist stress and handle pressure well, it is important to maintain a balance in life. So, no matter how absorbing or demanding your job may be, taking time out for relaxation – and not feeling guilty about it – is vital. Moderate exercise is helpful, provided you avoid becoming fanatical about it, as is sufficient rest and a healthy diet. Make sure that you also balance your own needs with those of other people. Stand up for yourself when necessary and talk about your own needs and feelings if you feel that they are being ignored.

▲ **Calming down**
The goal of meditation, which has been used for centuries to counteract the effects of stress, is to achieve a state of calm awareness. Among its many benefits are improved clarity and mental focus.

Shaping your own future
People who have an external locus of control often look to prediction therapies for answers to life, rather than taking responsibility themselves.

FEELING IN CONTROL

According to psychologists, people who believe they are in control of their own destinies handle pressure better than those who believe that fate deals the cards. People who think that hard work and perseverance achieve results are are said to have an internal "locus of control". These types prefer to take action themselves to solve problems and view success as a result of design rather than luck. People who believe that their lives are subject to a great deal of outside influence have an external "locus of control", and are less likely to take the initiative to solve problems themselves, preferring to leave matters to fate, or to someone else.

THRIVING ON THE PRESENT

Living in the here and now, or focusing on what is happening in the present, increases your resistance to stress. This is because when pressure occurs, you can deal with it more effectively when you are not distracted by worrying about past memories or imagining future disasters. When problems occur, you also need to be able to enlist the support of others, even if only to talk through problems. Build a strong social support network so that you can relax and laugh with friends when pressured – this is an ideal way to prevent stress.

HAVING A SENSE OF PURPOSE

With a strong sense of direction in life, you are far less likely to view minor pressures as a source of stress. When you are clear about your priorities and firm in your beliefs, you are able to see the bigger picture, rather than being sidetracked by minor irritations. If, for example, your priorities are to have a good family life and enjoy interesting work, then becoming stuck in a traffic jam may be irritating but will probably not bother you unduly. Think about what is important to you in life and develop your religious, spiritual, or philosophical beliefs to help maintain perspective in times of difficulty.

FOCUS POINT

- If you lack direction in life, take time out to write a list of all the things you would like to achieve.

Having fun ▶
When enjoying a family outing, banish all thoughts of work or domestic worries and simply have fun. Humour and a sense of playfulness are excellent stress inhibitors.

Assessing Your Pressure Levels

*E*valuate how well you are currently dealing with pressure by responding to the following statements. Mark the answers that are closest to your experience. Be as honest as you can: if your answer is "Never", mark Option 1; if it is "Always", mark Option 4; and so on. Add your scores together, and refer to the analysis for guidance.

Options

1. Never
2. Occasionally
3. Frequently
4. Always

How Do You Respond?

	1	2	3	4
1 When I feel pressure it makes me panicky.	☐	☐	☐	☐
2 When under pressure I drink more alcohol.	☐	☐	☐	☐
3 When under pressure I eat more.	☐	☐	☐	☐
4 I smoke more when under pressure.	☐	☐	☐	☐
5 I am a very competitive person.	☐	☐	☐	☐
6 I find it difficult to relax.	☐	☐	☐	☐
7 On holiday I become easily bored.	☐	☐	☐	☐
8 I have too much responsibility in my life.	☐	☐	☐	☐
9 I like to get things done quickly.	☐	☐	☐	☐

	1	2	3	4
10 I like to have lots of things going on.	☐	☐	☐	☐
11 I dislike having my routine disrupted.	☐	☐	☐	☐
12 I am not appreciated sufficiently by others.	☐	☐	☐	☐
13 I find it difficult to concentrate.	☐	☐	☐	☐
14 I have a tendency to forget things.	☐	☐	☐	☐
15 I never seem to have time to exercise.	☐	☐	☐	☐
16 I snap at people for no good reason.	☐	☐	☐	☐
17 I cannot find the time to relax.	☐	☐	☐	☐
18 My travel routine is unpredictable.	☐	☐	☐	☐

	1	2	3	4
19 I have to deal with difficult people.	☐	☐	☐	☐
20 I always set high standards for myself.	☐	☐	☐	☐
21 I tend to imagine the worst will happen.	☐	☐	☐	☐
22 I always take on responsibilities.	☐	☐	☐	☐
23 Other people take advantage of me.	☐	☐	☐	☐
24 I feel that my life is disorganized.	☐	☐	☐	☐
25 I am always losing things.	☐	☐	☐	☐

	1	2	3	4
26 I always feel that I have too much to do.	☐	☐	☐	☐
27 I seem to go from one crisis to another.	☐	☐	☐	☐
28 I tend to feel that delegating is risky.	☐	☐	☐	☐
29 I think that others are critical of me.	☐	☐	☐	☐
30 Slow service always annoys me.	☐	☐	☐	☐
31 I do not like saying "no" to people.	☐	☐	☐	☐
32 I do things at the last minute.	☐	☐	☐	☐

Analysis

When you have added up your scores, look at the analysis below to establish how pressured you really are. Then note which aspects of your life are causing you most and least pressure. You need to work on those areas that are causing most pressure.

32–64 At the moment, life seems to be relatively pressure-free. You may need to put yourself under a degree of pressure in order to feel challenged and motivated.

65–95 You are under moderate pressure and would benefit from making sure that you have the resources to cope effectively.

96–128 You are under a great deal of pressure and perhaps in danger of damaging your health or being overwhelmed.

I feel most pressured when:

_____

_____

_____

_____

I feel least pressured when:

_____

_____

_____

Preparing to Handle Pressure

To benefit from pressure, you need to be equipped to deal with it. Be positive, organized, communicative, and look after your health, and pressure will bring out the best in you.

Overcoming Worry

Excessive worrying wastes time and energy and makes it difficult to thrive under pressure. Understand why you worry, avoid doing so unnecessarily, and try to solve problems if possible. If you cannot resolve a situation, look for ways to distract yourself.

FOCUS POINT

● Use laughter as an antidote for anxiety – it distracts you from your current worries.

Useful Exercises

▶ Identify exactly what is worrying you by writing down your top five worries.

▶ Make a list of the good things in your life, such as a comfortable home, good health, or good friends.

▶ If you are unable to sleep, write down your worry. You will rest easier if you note the problem and plan to tackle it in the morning.

UNDERSTANDING WORRY

People often worry because they think that by fretting, they will prevent something bad from happening. If the outcome is bad, they may also feel less guilty and disappointed if they have worried about the matter. Sometimes people exaggerate problems in order to get attention. Worriers often predict the worst so that if and when things do go wrong, the reality is less frightening than they had anticipated. But while moderate worry can motivate you to work harder and create better solutions, excessive worry interferes with rational thinking and causes stress.

CHALLENGING WORRY

Worry often diverts attention away from a real concern. For example, a mother may distract herself from the dilemma of whether to return to work by worrying about how her children are doing at school. Challenge yourself as to why you are really worrying and what good it will do you. Imagine the very worst thing that could happen and calmly tell yourself that you can deal with it. Put your worries into context by asking yourself, "Will all this really matter in a year?".

66Drag your thoughts away from your troubles … by the ears, by the heels, or any other way you can manage it.99

Mark Twain

LIMITING WORRY

If you are beset by worries, set aside part of your day, say half an hour, as "worry time". Try to pick a time of day when you usually feel calm and positive. Devote that period to sitting down and making a list of niggling concerns. Then consider ways to deal with each worry on the list. If you find yourself worrying at other times during the day, postpone that worry until the allotted time.

Self-Talk

If you find yourself worrying excessively, use the affirmations below to help you develop a more positive outlook.

66*I am an optimist. I will focus on the good things in my life.*99

66*Worrying about a situation will not improve things. It's just a waste of my valuable time and energy.*99

66*There is no point in worrying about situations that are beyond my control.*99

66*The more I worry, the worse I will feel, so I will stop right now.*99

66*Whatever happens, I know I can cope with it.*99

◀ **Accomplishing a task**
Because worrying always involves uncertainty, it is a good idea to occupy yourself with a useful activity, even if it is simply going shopping. This helps you feel that you are doing something constructive.

RESOLVING WORRIES

Deal with one worry at a time to avoid feeling overwhelmed. Ask yourself what you can do to change a worrying situation. The fact is that there is almost always something that can be done. Let go of the worry and focus on finding a solution. List all the options open to you to help you decide on a course of action. You may find it helpful to imagine how other people, such as friends or colleagues, might deal with the problem. Or you may wish to discuss your worry with someone else to help you clarify it and find an approach to solving it.

> 66 Worry often gives a small thing a big shadow. 99
>
> Swedish proverb

Telephones bank to check status of personal loan application

FOCUS POINTS

● Note that only nine per cent of worries are thought to relate to issues that warrant valid concern.

● Avoid wasting time thinking about minor problems and trivialities.

▲ **Taking positive action**
Worrying that there are insufficient funds in your bank account to pay bills will not resolve the problem or lessen the worry. By applying for a loan, you take positive steps to solve the situation.

Things to Do	**Things to Avoid**
✓ Do focus on the positive – on what you have achieved and what is positive and good in your life.	✗ Avoid focusing on the negative and allowing yourself to believe that there is nothing good in your life.
✓ Do say to yourself that you would prefer to do, rather than must do, something. Tell yourself, "I would rather finish this job before dinner, but it isn't the end of the world if I don't".	✗ Avoid giving yourself "should" messages, such as "I should look after everybody all the time" or "I should never get anything wrong at work". These only make you feel inadequate.
✓ Do try to think logically about what is happening in a situation and whether there is evidence to support the way in which you are reacting.	✗ Avoid allowing an emotional response to govern your interpretation of a situation, for example, "I feel frightened, so it must be dangerous to be here".

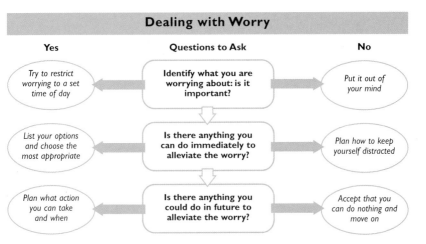

Dealing with Worry

Yes	Questions to Ask	No
Try to restrict worrying to a set time of day	**Identify what you are worrying about: is it important?**	Put it out of your mind
List your options and choose the most appropriate	**Is there anything you can do immediately to alleviate the worry?**	Plan how to keep yourself distracted
Plan what action you can take and when	**Is there anything you could do in future to alleviate the worry?**	Accept that you can do nothing and move on

ACCEPTING THE INEVITABLE

If you conclude that there is nothing that you can do about a problem, stop worrying and accept the fact. Look for ways to prevent yourself from dwelling on the unavoidable. If you know you are going to be troubled by a situation, do whatever you can to distract yourself. If the worry is likely to be long-term, take up a new hobby or join a club. If it is short-term, anything from an invigorating swim to a relaxed evening at home can take your mind off your worries. Laughter also lifts the spirits, so watch a comedy on television, hire a funny video, or spend time with friends who make you laugh.

▲ **Distracting yourself from your worries**
Go to the gym or take a favourite exercise class to help you relax. When you indulge in a pleasant activity and disengage yourself from a problem, solutions can often occur "out of the blue".

Setting Up Your Support System

People sometimes feel isolated when they are under pressure, and they believe that no one understands what they are going through. Build constructive relationships with people and allow them to offer you support to reduce this feeling.

66A friend may well be reckoned to be the masterpiece of nature. 99

Ralph Waldo Emerson

FOCUS POINTS

● Be open about your feelings – simply discussing your emotions with a good friend can alleviate your anxiety.

● Talk to a counsellor if you feel that your family and friends cannot offer the right kind of support.

ARRANGING SUPPORT

Having friends or relatives with whom you can talk things through helps ease the pressure on you. Discussing issues enables you to keep a sense of perspective because others are able to ask objective questions and challenge you when your fears are exaggerated. Choose your confidants carefully, bearing in mind that some people may feel embarrassed or distressed if you openly express your emotions. Ask your close friends whether they would mind your talking to them about your problems. Explain that you will not necessarily be looking for guidance but for a sympathetic ear. Make it clear from the outset that you will be delighted to reciprocate by listening sympathetically yourself whenever your friend feels the need to talk.

◀ **Building relationships**
Arrange fun outings to treat friends who have been particularly supportive. This is a good way to build deeper rapport and thank people for "being there" for you.

ACCEPTING HELP

If you think of yourself as capable, responsible, and resourceful in a crisis, and you prefer solve your own problems rather than delegate or seek help from others, you may be suffering from the "be-strong" tendency. This can deter you from seeking help and make you appear invulnerable to others. But it is important to realize that coping alone only increases the pressure on you. If people usually approach you for help, do you feel that your advice is usually helpful? What makes you think that other people cannot help you in the same way? Confide in people you trust, and if you feel vulnerable, admit it. No one can be strong all the time, and if you attempt to be, you will simply be putting yourself under unnecessary pressure.

Fact File

People with good support systems (friends, families, colleagues) handle pressure better than those without support. Friends who are good listeners and give emotional support are of most help in a situation that cannot be changed. Those who problem-solve and provide information are of most help when a problem can be rectified.

Is called to crisis meeting at office but is due to pick up children from school

Calls friend to ask her to pick up children

Arrives at work in time to solve problem

Rushes to pick up children herself and take them over to her mother's

Arrives at office, but too late to resolve anything

▲ Asking for help

In this scenario, there are two outcomes for a mother facing a work crisis. By failing to ask for help, she arrives too late for a critical meeting, but a call to a friend ensures that she reaches the office in time to save the day.

Being Organized

W*hen under pressure, it helps to be in organized and orderly surroundings because this makes you feel more in control. Decide which areas of your home most need organizing, clear your space of clutter, and encourage others to be tidier, too.*

WORKING OUT A SYSTEM

Evaluate each room in turn to identify its specific problems. When you are in the kitchen, for example, it is easier to remember that you keep losing your keys because you have no specific place to hang them. Make sure that items in regular use are easily accessible and those that are rarely used are moved to the back of cupboards, or out of the way. If you never use an item, either give it to someone, recycle it, or throw it away. Think about investing in innovative storage solutions, such wardrobe organizers, shoe holders, or box files.

Organizing your files ▶
Filing important personal documents makes it far easier to run your life. If you need to check an insurance policy, for example, you will know exactly where to find it.

FOCUS POINT

● Sort through one drawer, cupboard, or office area at a time to avoid leaving jobs unfinished.

Useful Exercises

▶ Adopt the "new for old" principle. Every time you buy a new item, throw away an old one.

▶ Before you empty cupboards, decide on a system – such as organizing separate bags for charity goods, rubbish, and items that need repairing. Put possessions to keep to one side.

▶ Read up on feng shui – it may inspire you to organize your living space in certain ways in an effort to improve your health, wealth, or love life!

Files only essential records that will be needed in future

Lays memories to rest by packing away treasured souvenirs

CLEARING CLUTTER

Make a fresh start and gain a sense of control by clearing out clutter. This is especially useful when you want to change the atmosphere of a space after a traumatic event or when you want to use a room for a different purpose. Clutter in your personal environment can mirror internal chaos. Your possessions can anchor you in the past or your current situation and prevent you from moving forward. Decide on your goals for the next two years and clear your space accordingly, throwing out anything that does not relate to your immediate plans.

◀ **Lightening your load**
Memorabilia that no longer has any relevance to your life should be thrown out. This will enable you to put the past behind you and make the most of the present.

ENCOURAGING TIDINESS

When you live or work with other people who are untidy, it can be very difficult to maintain order. Encourage tidiness in others by leading by example. If you do not clear up after yourself, you cannot expect others to be tidy either. Gain cooperation by tailoring your reorganization to their priorities. For example, if you live with someone who owns hundreds of compact discs, they may feel more inclined to keep them tidy if they have their own CD rack with space for the entire collection. Explain to children that their toys should be put away properly so that they are not broken – but avoid becoming too fussy about children's clutter or you risk putting yourself under unnecessary pressure.

FOCUS POINT

● Remember that if you allow your living space to get out of control, the chances are that your life will follow suit.

▼ **Gaining cooperation**
When someone is very untidy, you may need to tackle them about their behaviour. Agree that they can do as they like in their private space but reach a compromise on a level of neatness in shared areas. Avoid the temptation to clean up after someone, or you will find yourself always doing it.

Explain how untidiness is affecting you	Distinguish between shared and private space	Agree on a level of tidiness in shared areas

Improving Your Time Management

Good time management reduces pressure, indecisiveness, and confusion, and improves your quality of life. Learn how to plan your time more effectively so that you can give yourself more freedom to do all the things you really want to do.

Allocates time off to play golf

EXAMINING USE OF TIME

If you consistently find yourself rushing, being late, or having no time for leisure pursuits, you may be trying to cram in too much activity. As a starting point, look at how you divide up your day at the moment. Do you allocate time to activities that make little contribution to your overall goals? Do you waste a lot of time? Could you streamline your schedule to make life easier? Perhaps you are trying to fulfil too many roles? Assess whether you can drop less important activities for a while.

▲ **Analyzing your schedule**
Review how you have spent the past month. Did you give yourself time for recreation, relationships, relaxation, and family, as well as work? If not, work out your priorities and allocate sufficient time to them next month.

FOCUS POINTS

● Avoid overfilling your timetable – always allow yourself some slack.

● Schedule time each day to switch off; pick a quiet period that fits in with your personal energy rhythm and work obligations.

ORGANIZING YOUR TIME

Write a "Things to do" list and prioritize the items. Most people tend to do trivial or minor things first and never get around to more important tasks. Break down larger tasks into small, manageable pieces so that you are not tempted to avoid a project because you have limited time or are unsure where to begin. Consider whether you can eliminate any tasks – do you really need to weed the garden every week, for example? Try to delegate more. Ask yourself whether anyone else can do the task, or at least share it with you.

Slowing down
*Stop what you are doing every couple
of hours throughout the day and take a
minimum of 10 minutes for a break.*

STAYING IN CONTROL

Some people respond well to pressure, often
producing their best work when they know there is
no time to waste. They enjoy this feeling, and it
helps them to feel more in control. This sense of
time urgency can, however, become an obsession,
and if you are addicted to last-minute deadlines,
you will often take on far too much in order to
feed the addiction. To overcome these habits and
avoid the risk of burnout, increase your leisure
and relaxation time. Stagger your deadlines,
if necessary by planning interim targets along the
way in order to prevent last-minute panics.

ENJOYING FREE TIME

One reason why people fail to make
the most of their free time is that
they schedule favourite activities
for the end of the day, thinking
that this will motivate them to
work through their other tasks
more quickly. However, what
happens in reality is that
in a busy schedule you are
unlikely to reach this reward
activity and may feel cheated
as a result. It is much more
effective to schedule time
earlier in the day, which is
when you are likely to feel at
your best and gain maximum
benefit from the activity.

*Feels more
creative early
in the morning*

Finding extra time ▶
*Getting up slightly earlier and
engaging in a favourite activity
before you do anything else can lift
your mood and put you in a positive
frame of mind for the rest of the day.*

Exercising for Resilience

When you are in good physical shape, you feel fit for life – and all its pressures. Get into the habit of exercising by finding activities that challenge and satisfy you. Stay motivated by setting realistic goals and rewarding yourself regularly.

MAKING EXERCISE A HABIT

To gain maximum benefits from exercise, you should build up your fitness gradually and keep exercising regularly. As well as taking into account your age and fitness level, any exercise routine needs to suit your personality and lifestyle if you are to stick to it. If you are particularly sociable, for instance, you may wish to join a swimming or running club. If flexibility is important to you, being able to go to a nearby gym at any time and in any weather may be more appealing. The best forms of exercise for countering the negative effects of pressure are rhythmic and gradual, rather than frenetic and highly competitive. Brisk walking, swimming, and cycling are effective, inexpensive types of exercise that can easily be built into daily routines.

FOCUS POINTS

● Use exercise both to increase your sense of well-being and to keep yourself in shape.

● Make sure that you avoid becoming obsessed with exercise – that would create its own pressure.

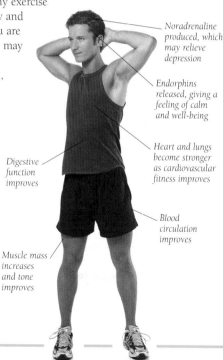

Noradrenaline produced, which may relieve depression

Endorphins released, giving a feeling of calm and well-being

Heart and lungs become stronger as cardiovascular fitness improves

Digestive function improves

Blood circulation improves

Muscle mass increases and tone improves

Improving health and fitness ▶
Regular exercise strengthens your immune system, protecting you against illness, and builds physical stamina. It also increases energy levels, helps to maintain a healthy weight, and promotes restful sleep.

STAYING MOTIVATED

Having realistic goals will help you get the most from your exercise routine. Keep your programme interesting by interspersing visits to the gym with a cycle ride, run, or walk if you find yourself growing bored. Consider keeping an exercise diary so that you can record each exercise session, noting what you achieved and how you felt. This can provide a boost when you look back after a few weeks and see how much you have progressed. Focus on how much better you feel after exercising, and plan rewards, too. If you have worked hard in the gym, treat yourself to a sauna afterwards.

At a Glance

- An exercise routine needs to be planned around your habits, interests, and lifestyle.

- Exercising for at least 20 minutes three times a week significantly improves health and fitness levels.

- Setting realistic targets and planning rewards will motivate you to build on your successes as you increase your fitness.

◀ **Finding an exercise partner**
Make exercise more fun by teaming up with a friend and working out together. When you can share your experiences and spur each other on, getting into shape can be doubly enjoyable.

Benefiting from Different Types of Exercise

Type	Description	Benefits
Aerobic	Running, brisk walking, swimming, or other cardiovascular activity.	Strengthens heart and increases lung capacity and efficiency.
Anaerobic	Lifting weights, resistance training.	Builds muscle, strengthens bones, improves core strength.
Stretching	Pilates, yoga, t'ai chi, some forms of dance exercise.	Increases flexibility, improves muscle tone.

Eating and Drinking Well

Good nutrition keeps the body in peak condition, helping us feel well and full of energy in times of pressure. Plan a healthy diet, eat regular meals, and drink plenty of water to maintain good health. But do enjoy your food, too – take pleasure in preparing and savouring what you eat.

FOCUS POINT

● Monitor what you consume and when to reveal bad habits that have crept into your diet – and plan how to change them.

Fact File

Fats are a key component of many cells in the body. However, because of their high calorie content and associated health risks, fats should make up no more than 30 per cent of your daily calorie intake.

CHOOSING WISELY

A healthy diet will protect you from illness, improve your outlook, and make you feel equal to the pressures of everyday life. Try to eat five or six portions of fruit and vegetables every day – a portion being a palm-sized amount. A glass of juice counts as one portion. Wherever possible, buy organic products. Supplement fruit and vegetables with proteins such as fish, chicken, tofu (vegetable protein), and lean meat. Proteins produce the chemical serotonin, which promotes feelings of wellbeing. Eat plenty of complex carbohydrates such as pasta, rice, potatoes, and pulses. These contain magnesium, which also helps to alleviate depression. Try to avoid sweet, sugary snacks, which boost energy temporarily but will cause a slump later.

Eats slowly, and chews thoroughly to aid digestion

◀ **Eating breakfast**
The most important meal of the day, breakfast helps maintain energy and concentration. Eating breakfast is also thought to increase resistance to colds and flu.

Choosing the Best Stress-Resistor Foods

Nutrient	Properties	Sources
Vitamin A	Encourages cell growth and development, and defends against infections. Helps keep skin, hair, nails, and eyes healthy.	Oranges, grapefruit, apricots, peaches, apples, pears, melon, strawberries, carrots, beans, tomatoes, spinach, broccoli, eggs, cheese, butter, oily fish, liver.
Vitamin C	Promotes strong blood vessels and maintains gums, teeth, and bones. Also improves iron absorption and aids the immune system.	Lemons, oranges, grapefruit, strawberries, blackberries, raspberries, blackcurrants, gooseberries, kiwi fruit, mangoes, tomatoes, sweet peppers, broccoli, cabbage, spinach.
Vitamin E	Helps stimulate immune system and protects against heart disease. Also helps formation of red blood cells.	Asparagus, broccoli, kale, spinach, Brussels sprouts, avocados, eggs, olives, salmon, tuna, nuts, kidney beans, vegetable oils, brown rice, wheatgerm, wholemeal bread.
Selenium	Plays a role in preventing cell damage and stimulates the immune system. It may reduce the risk of developing some forms of cancer.	Brazil nuts, fish, mushrooms, wheatgerm, wholegrains, bran, offal, lamb, beef, chicken, turkey, duck, shellfish, white fish, tuna, milk, butter, cheese, lentils, avocados, garlic.
Zinc	Assists wound healing and maintains health of skin and hair. Aids digestion and metabolism. Helps keep reproductive system healthy.	Milk, butter, cheese, peanuts, sunflower seeds, oysters, fish, shellfish, liver, beef, lamb, chicken, turkey, wheatgerm, wholegrains.

THE VALUE OF ANTIOXIDANTS

Antioxidants reduce free radicals produced in the body during the digestion process. Free radicals damage cell membranes, disrupt the immune system, and are believed to encourage cancer cells to grow. Antioxidants are known to boost the immune system, making it more resistant to the damaging effects of stress. Antioxidants are found in vitamins A (as beta-carotene), C, and E, and in selenium and bioflavonoids (chemicals that strengthen the capillaries).

Sources of antioxidants
Both broccoli and oranges contain beta-carotene and vitamin C and are valuable sources of antioxidants.

TIMING YOUR MEALS

Aim to eat five small meals a day, rather than three large ones. This keeps the blood sugar level steady so that your energy is maintained evenly throughout the day, rather than rising or falling sharply. Alternatively, have a small, healthy snack mid-morning and at teatime. Avoid skipping meals during the day, and then having a huge dinner in the evening, since this puts the digestive system under pressure. Eating a large meal just before going to bed can also disrupt your sleep, so if you feel hungry, have a light snack only.

Fact File

Water is essential for digestion, the elimination of waste, and many other bodily functions. The human body is made up of two-thirds water, with bones being made up of 20 per cent water and brains and muscles consisting of 75 per cent water. For these reasons, drinking enough water is fundamental to good health.

▲ **Drinking water regularly**
Aim to drink at least eight glasses (or 1.5 litres) of water per day – if you start to feel thirsty, this is a sign that your body is already dehydrated.

CHOOSING WHAT TO DRINK

Drink water rather than sugary soft drinks or caffeinated coffee to keep up energy levels, promote clear thinking, and improve your appearance. Carry a small bottle of mineral water in your bag, and keep a large one close to your work-station. It is especially important to drink plenty of water during and after exercise to make up for loss of fluid through sweating. When you are drinking alcohol, alternate alcoholic drinks with glasses of water to reduce the risk of dehydration. Herbal and fruit teas, available in many flavours, are a healthy alternative to caffeinated drinks.

LOOKING AFTER YOURSELF

By taking time to choose and buy fresh food, you are making your well-being, and that of your family, a priority in your life – and this, in itself, will boost your self-esteem. In giving thought to what you eat and its nutritional value, you are more likely to prepare healthy meals and, consequently, you will find that weight control is easier. Rather than punishing yourself through depriving yourself of specific foods, you can take the much more positive approach of nurturing yourself through eating food that is doing you and your family good.

ENJOYING FOOD

Good food is part of a general enjoyment of life, and it is important to take time to sit and savour your meals, rather than grabbing a snack on the hop. Preparing food can be very relaxing – there is something reassuring about the rhythmic chopping and stirring that food preparation involves. And, of course, sharing food with family and friends is a good way of socializing and unwinding. Often, meal times are the only opportunity for busy families to get together.

Useful Exercises

▶ Make a comprehensive list of healthy foods when you go shopping – and stick to it.

▶ At mealtimes, stop eating just before you get a feeling of being full. Notice how much more energy you have than usual.

▶ Prepare nutritious salads and snacks to take to work with you to keep up your healthy eating.

▲ **Cooking sensibly**
Experiment with healthier, low-fat versions of calorie-laden recipes, such as creamy pasta sauces. Substitute more vegetables and herbs for an equally delicious meal.

Learning to Relax

Thriving under pressure involves knowing how and when to unwind. Choose activities that refresh you, do them regularly, and make use of breathing and relaxation techniques to combat stress and encourage a good night's sleep.

Loose, comfortable clothing is good for walking

TAKING TIME OUT

Do you have any hobbies that you enjoy and can do regularly? Sports like golf, sailing, and walking demand energy but are relaxing because they transfer you into a different environment. Look for an activity that provides a complete contrast to what you are doing the rest of the time. For example, for those working in offices in front of a computer screen, doing domestic chores, such as cooking, cleaning, or gardening, can be extremely therapeutic. If, on the other hand, you work, or spend a lot of time at home, you may find it more relaxing to get out of the house – even if only to go shopping or see a movie.

▲ **Walking the dog**
Exercising your pet can be the perfect way to unwind. Go at your own pace, breathe in fresh air, observe the scenery, and let your mind wander as you walk.

FOCUS POINTS

- Unless you are a night owl, an hour's rest before midnight is usually worth two afterwards.
- If you cannot sleep, try to avoid worrying about it – just resting in bed will do you some good.

SLEEPING WELL

An inability to relax can disrupt sleeping patterns, especially when pressure is intense and your mind is still racing when it is time to go to bed. To help you sleep, avoid caffeine after lunch and cut out alcohol altogether. Aim to go to bed at the same time every evening, when you feel moderately tired. Do not stay up until you feel exhausted because this creates more tension. Try eating a banana, which contains tryptophan (a natural relaxant), mid-evening. A bath and a warm milky drink before going to bed may also help you sleep.

AVOIDING TRANQUILLIZERS

Tranquillizers are a family of drugs prescribed to help control anxiety and tension and to aid sleep. Sedatives depress mental activity and alertness. However, psychological dependence is common in long-term users, for whom a life without the drug may seem very daunting. Some tranquillizers also have unpleasant side effects such as drowsiness, appetite changes, dry mouth, dizziness, and poor coordination, which can start to affect quality of life.

Using natural sleeping aids
Herbal preparations can often help with short-term insomnia, and there is no risk of dependence.

Relaxing the Mind

Sit down quietly and close your eyes for about 5 minutes

⬇

Listen to your breathing and focus on slowing it down

⬇

Visualize cool air coming in and warm air being exhaled from your body

⬇

Imagine the cares of the day being expelled from your body as you breathe out

RELAXING THE BODY

If you are feeling tense, try a relaxation exercise. Lie in a warm room where you will not be disturbed. You may want to play relaxing music. Focus on the toes of your right foot, clenching and relaxing them three times. Each time you relax, imagine that your toes are liquid or molten, like oil or gold. Repeat the process with your left toes, and then begin to move gradually up the body from the legs, up the torso, and to the shoulders and neck, tensing and relaxing until you reach your face and scalp. Finally, concentrate on your forehead, clearing any thoughts from your mind.

▼ **Relaxing your muscles**
Clench and relax all your muscles in turn, working from your feet up to the top of your head. Imagine the tension floating out of your body every time you relax.

Thoughts are calm and relaxed

Breathing is slow and regular

Legs are relaxed and comfortable

Coping with Everyday Pressures

Everyone has to cope with difficult situations and people in life, as well as handle routine irritants, such as commuting. Learn how to negotiate these challenges successfully.

Responding to Demands

When people apply pressure by asking you to do things for them, it is often very difficult to answer "no". Consider whether you can, or want, to do what is asked, and if not, learn how to refuse a request effectively.

> "Honest disagreement is often a good sign of progress."
>
> Mahatma Gandhi

FOCUS POINTS

● Practise saying "no" in front of a mirror so that you feel more comfortable about saying it.

● If someone puts you on the spot, avoid reacting straight away and ask for time to consider what they are asking of you.

ANALYZING YOUR FEELINGS

People who have been brought up to be conciliatory may find it difficult to refuse the requests of others. They may ignore – or fail to even notice – their "gut" reaction to a request. When someone asks you for something, do you answer in a way that will please them, or do you reply honestly? Do you feel used, or do you feel you have to comply, for example? What feeling are you experiencing? Are you reminded of a similar situation in the past? By listening to and analyzing how you feel, you are less likely to give in to a request that you would really rather refuse.

SAYING "NO" EFFECTIVELY

If you want to say "no", then say so clearly. You do not have to make excuses or to justify yourself unless you think it is appropriate to give some kind of explanation. For example, you might say, "No, I can't, because I'm meeting a friend". Remember that it is not the person you are rejecting – you are merely turning down his or her request. Avoid giving too many reasons for saying "no", since this will sound more like a list of excuses. If you feel uncomfortable with a curt "no", you could soften the negative by saying "We could, but...", or "Maybe another time…".

At a Glance

● Learning to say "no" helps you avoid circumstances that create pressure, such as lending people money or having unwanted guests.

● Being more assertive helps prevent anger and resentment from building up.

● There are times when you do not have to be cooperative.

Getting Your Message Across

State directly what you are prepared or not prepared to do

⬇

Compose a sentence showing you have considered the other person's feelings

⬇

In a firm voice, repeat the first statement each time the request is made

⬇

Occasionally insert your expression of empathy when appropriate

⬇

Repeat the message until the other person accepts it

Realizes that her mind is made up

Is calm and polite, and maintains direct eye contact while refusing request

▲ Being convincing

If someone tries to put pressure on you, show that you are sensitive to their position but that you will not be moved from yours. Speak slowly and clearly so that you sound resolute, and keep your voice soft to avoid sounding aggressive.

FOCUS POINTS

● Know what you want, be sure it is fair, and ask for it clearly.

● If you have been coerced into saying "yes", feel free to change your mind.

SAYING "YES"

If you want say "yes", be clear about what it is you are agreeing to. You may want to modify what you are prepared to offer, or agree that you will comply with the request but subject to conditions of your own. For example, you might say "Yes, I'm happy to babysit, but I can't do Saturday night because I'm going out. I could babysit on Friday". Or you might agree to pick up some shopping for a neighbour provided they look after the children.

POSTPONING A DECISION

If you are unsure about whether to say "yes" or "no" to a request, make sure that you do not feel pressured to comply just to avoid unpleasantness. Ask yourself, "What are the rewards for the other person, and what are the rewards for me?" "Will I be doing this because I really want to?" "Do I have the time to help, or am I already under pressure?" You may need to ask for more information, or more time, in order to reach a decision.

Manager asks colleague to take on extra work

Explains he is already working late to complete projects

Making your case ▶
If you are asked to do more than you feel is appropriate at work, make sure that a superior understands how hard you are working and why you feel it is unreasonable to ask you to take on more.

Things to Do

✓ Do ask for further details if someone is being vague about what they are asking of you.

✓ Do make sure that you have enough information to make your decision.

✓ Do express your opinion honestly – while letting other people know that you suspect they may not like it.

Things to Avoid

✗ Avoid agreeing to do things just because you are afraid of seeming selfish or uncooperative.

✗ Avoid rushing into any decision – take as much time as you need.

✗ Avoid keeping your opinions to yourself, particularly when you feel strongly about something.

Self-Talk

Use the following affirmations to help you speak up and overcome passive tendencies.

**My opinion is worth hearing and can be valuable to others.**

**The more I stand up for myself, the higher my self-esteem will be.**

**Expressing an honest opinion can be a generous act.**

SAYING WHAT YOU THINK

It is important to express your opinion honestly, even though you may risk upsetting people, or face the prospect that they will start an argument. So if you believe that a request is unreasonable, you should say so. Failure to express opinions leads to "passive-aggressive" behaviour when anger and frustration at being unable to speak openly are manifested in sullen silence, nagging, blaming, or manipulative back-stabbing. Passive-aggressive behaviour also has a detrimental effect on health because pent-up frustration or anger can take its toll on the immune system.

BEING SENSITIVE

If you plan to express an opinion that may upset someone, choose the place and time carefully. You may not want to voice it in a public arena. Give balance to your opinions by expressing appreciative points first, for example, "I realize that you are working extremely hard at the moment … but I feel resentful that you never help with the cooking any more". Avoid name-calling or using hurtful labels because this will simply put the other person on the defensive. Instead describe their behaviour and the effect it is having on you. Sometimes, expressing opinions about things that cannot be changed may not be worthwhile – remember it is just your view of the situation.

Criticizing constructively ▷
State your feelings, explaining why you are hurt or inconvenienced by the other person's behaviour, and state how you would like that behaviour to change.

**Pleasant people are just as real as horrible people.**

John Braine

Handling Conflict

E veryone has to face conflict with
friends, family, or colleagues at some
point. Confrontations can be stressful, but
you can relieve the pressure by remaining
calm and in control, and by standing up for
yourself and being more assertive.

*Is angry with neighbour
who has registered
objections to her
planning application*

*Listens to
complaints
before
responding*

STAYING CALM

It is important to remain calm in a confrontation
in order to listen properly and think rationally. Try
to separate yourself and the other person from the
issue and concentrate on the facts. Listen carefully
to what is being said and try to make plenty of eye
contact to build empathy and give yourself
maximum opportunity to read someone's
reactions. If you feel nervous or
defensive, focus on reassuring
and involving the other person.

◀ Clarifying important points
*In order to keep track of the conversation
and resolve the issues, check that you have
understood what has been said by stopping
to repeat and clarify key points.*

Fact File

One technique for handling
conflict is called neutralizing,
which is taking the "sting" out
of words by paraphrasing what
has been said. For example, if
someone says, "I can't stand
my boss", you reply, "So, you
want to talk about improving
relations with your manager?"

LOOKING FOR COMPROMISE

Try to find a win-win outcome, or one from which
both parties will gain. Think about what you want
and what the other person wants and try to give
them something. To break a deadlock, look for
any issue you can agree on, from a small detail –
such as the time you both have to discuss the
issue – to a big principle – that the issue is one of
fairness, for example. This will improve the mood
of a negotiation so it becomes more conciliatory.

USING ASSERTIVE BODY LANGUAGE

In times of conflict, it is helpful to be as physically relaxed as possible. Avoid quick, jerky movements, and defensive or aggressive posturing. Try to appear as open and accessible as possible to indicate that you are prepared to listen. Angle your body slightly towards the other person to signal a willingness to communicate and build rapport. Avoid crossing either your arms or legs because these are "barrier" gestures that convey defensiveness. Acknowledge the other person's opinions through nodding and keeping eye contact to show that you are listening. Explain that you do not necessarily agree with what they are saying – useful phrases include "I would need to go away and think about that", or "possibly".

Open expression

Front of the body open and unprotected

Hands lightly clasped

Relaxed stance

Adopting more assertive body language ▶
Stand firm and take up plenty of space, keeping the front of the body relatively open and unprotected, and leaning forwards slightly to convey a desire for involvement.

Useful Exercises

▶ Practise breathing deeply. Then, as you exhale, try projecting your voice across the room.

▶ Practise voice projection by enunciating every consonant clearly and speaking more loudly than usual.

▶ If your throat feels constricted, just try yawning a few times (discreetly) to stretch and relax those tight muscles.

SOUNDING ASSERTIVE

To convey strength and clarity, your tone of voice needs to be strong and clear. Nervous voices are weak and wobbly in tone and imply that you can be swayed to someone else's point of view. In order to sound more definite and resolved, make sure that you are breathing properly, inhaling deeply into the lungs. You can practise sounding definite by dropping your pitch. Make a strong statement out loud, such as "No, I do not want to do that". As you come to the end of the phrase, make a firm downward movement with your hand. You will find that your pitch drops too, so that you convey firm authority.

43

Dealing with Difficult Behaviour

Most people have to deal with difficult behaviour at some point, so being forearmed with tactics to deflect it will relieve the pressure. Learn how to handle common forms of difficult behaviour, such as negativity and manipulation.

HANDLING NEGATIVITY

People who are always negative about your ideas like to see themselves as realists who are more in touch with life than you are. They also enjoy making people look inferior. Announce that you are about to start on a fitness regime and this type of individual is likely to point out that last time you joined a gym you went only four times. Simply remain cheerful and take note of their views, but avoid appearing to be deflated. Remember that you do not have to agree with the negative comments. Try disarming negative people by saying that you want to hear their views on an idea because you know you can rely on them to list all the pitfalls.

Remaining cheerful ▶
Often, the purpose of negativity is to deflate and belittle another person, so if you are on the receiving end of such comments, deflect them by remaining resolutely cheerful and positive.

FOCUS POINTS

● When someone makes a personal attack on you, deflect it with humour rather than allow it to make you angry.

● Try repeating a negative comment back to its source to underline just how destructive it is.

RISING ABOVE CRITICISM

The best tactic to use with people who criticize destructively is to depersonalize the criticism by viewing it as interesting feedback. Comments such as "That's interesting to know" show that you have heard the criticism, but are not necessarily accepting it, or responding emotionally. When the criticism is sarcastic, check that you understand what the person is implying, by paraphrasing what they said back to them. Encourage them to think about what they have said with a query such as, "That's an interesting viewpoint. Why would you say that?" So rather than giving them a wounded reaction, you enter into a discussion that aims at clarifying meaning and at the same time highlights their negative tactics.

> **FOCUS POINT**
>
> ● Consider whether your critics are in fact frustrated by their failure to meet their own high standards.

▼ **Challenging relentless critics**
If someone continually criticizes you, let them know how their behaviour is affecting you, and warn them of the consequences if they continue. You may wish to put some distance between yourself and the critic, for example, or even end a relationship.

| Describe the criticism you keep receiving | ▸▸▸ | Disclose how it makes you feel, for example, "hurt" | ▸▸▸ | Predict what you will do if the criticism continues |

TACKLING UNRESPONSIVENESS

When people show little response to those who want feedback and encouragement, they are being difficult by deliberately withholding a reaction. To encourage them to communicate, you may need to be direct. Use a request such as, "I would like a clearer idea of your views on this". If you still do not get a response, let them know that you find them hard to "read" and need clear feedback from them.

Encouraging a reaction ▶
When a colleague is failing to give you feedback, put your ideas down on paper so that they have something physical to engage with, and ask whether you could set a date to discuss your suggestions.

Agrees to look at ideas and get back to employee

Presents ideas in writing to manager

FOCUS POINT

● View dealing with difficult behaviour as a way of developing your skills as an amateur psychologist.

PLAYING DOWN A DRAMA

If you are in difficult circumstances, beware of people who take any opportunity to talk about your plight and over-sympathize with you. Some people thrive on drama and even relish others' misfortunes because they make them feel better about themselves. Try to avoid being drawn into discussion with such people. If they persist in trying to talk to you, reply to inquiries succinctly, giving a minimum of information. Bear in mind too that some people use drama to get their own way. For example, they may try to persuade you to agree to a request by telling you that their life could be ruined if you refuse to help them out.

Sympathetic colleague feels obliged to act as counsellor

◀ **Handling dramatics**
Make it clear that you will not put up with dramatics. Empathize and wish the person luck with resolving a difficulty but explain that you will not be able to help them yourself.

DEALING WITH PUT-DOWNS

People who are insecure often try to diminish other people's achievements or attributes in order to make themselves look and feel more important. If you have an Achille's heel, you can be sure that they will identify and draw attention to it in order to undermine you. Deal with this type of behaviour by pretending that you are unaffected. "I was never very good at spelling" would be the best response to someone who points out a flaw in your document, for example, or "My cooking has always been a bit hit-or-miss", to someone who speaks unfavourably about a meal you have prepared. The realization that you cannot be hurt by put-downs will deter people who use them.

At a Glance

● Having a positive, cheerful attitude is a good way to deter negative or critical comments.

● Instead of feeling wounded when you receive criticism, you should ask critics to explain themselves.

● If someone is too agitated or being too difficult to listen, it may sometimes be wiser to walk away.

● Persistent difficult behaviour should always be challenged.

COPING WITH YOUR EMOTIONS

When other people are being difficult or aggressive towards you, you are likely to feel hurt or scared. Stay calm so that you can deal with the situation effectively. Try to ignore physical reactions, such as fluttering in the stomach or clammy hands, and concentrate on breathing slowly, listening to what is being said, and keeping your body language open. Ask open questions to help you identify the cause of their hostility and negotiate a solution.

Dealing with anger
If someone is shouting, there is little point in trying to talk. Tell them you will discuss the issue once they have calmed down.

FOCUS POINT

● Remind yourself that people may be behaving in strange or difficult ways because they are unhappy.

CHALLENGING DIFFICULT BEHAVIOUR

When people persist in being difficult, you will have to ask them to stop. Plan carefully what you intend to say beforehand by writing a script. Be polite, concise, and explain clearly what you need. Begin with "I want" or "I would like", describe the nature of the problem, how it affects you, how you feel about it, and what you want to change. Be firm but be willing to listen to their point of view and explore solutions. Consider whether you need to compromise and change your attitude in order to help them alter their difficult behaviour.

Explains how difficult behaviour is affecting her

▲ **Asking someone to stop**
If you need to speak to someone about their difficult behaviour, warn them first about what you are going to say, so that they have a moment to collect themselves, then explain your feelings.

Useful Exercises

▶ Practise enunciating and stressing important words.

▶ Look at your behaviour from the other person's perspective. Are you their "difficult person"?

▶ Work out and write down what your "difficult person" is hoping to gain from his or her behaviour.

Dealing with Self-Imposed Pressure

People who put themselves under constant pressure to achieve more, yet never feel satisfied, risk damaging their physical and mental health. Learn to recognize when you are asking too much of yourself, and accept your limitations.

RECOGNIZING THE SIGNS

Everyone wants to do their best, and a degree of perfectionism is motivational – but it is important to know where to draw the line. If you feel isolated, this may be because you are giving the impression that you can manage perfectly well without help. Perfectionists find it difficult to make decisions because they feel that they never have enough information to choose between options. They also criticize those who cannot live up to their own high standards and blame others for their problems because they are unable to accept that they are at fault.

Lists things to do for the day and sets a time limit for each

Are You Too Perfectionist?

Tick the statements that you think apply to you.

- I believe that people will think less of me if I make a mistake. ☐
- I push myself to meet my own high standards. ☐
- I am good at spotting mistakes made by others. ☐
- I am attracted to people who share my high standards. ☐
- I take pride in being thorough. ☐
- I keep a tight rein on my emotions. ☐

Analysis The more statements you have ticked, the greater your tendency towards perfectionism.

◀ **Being realistic**
When planning tasks for the day, avoid trying to achieve too much because you will set yourself up for disappointment. Prioritize the important jobs and give yourself the satisfaction of completing what you set out to do.

REALIZING YOUR LIMITS

It is important to realize that sometimes just being "good enough" will suffice. Your value as a human being lies in who you are, rather than in what you achieve. Place more value on enthusiasm and creativity instead of striving for achievement. Accept that you cannot expect perfection in every area of life. Relationships are not always harmonious, and you cannot always look perfect and have a perfect home and family, too. Show your vulnerability and confide in close friends or family if you feel inadequate. Ask yourself if there is one area in which it is important for you to continue to be your very best. Can you settle for being just good enough in some of the other areas?

Savouring the moment ▶

In roles such as being a parent, nobody achieves perfection. Try to simply enjoy what you are doing in the here and now rather than concentrating on what you hope to achieve from it.

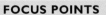

Focuses on having fun with the children rather than on cooking the perfect meal

Self-Talk

Accept that you can learn from mistakes and get it right the next time. Tell yourself:

❝*I have done the best I can and that's good enough for me.*❞

❝*Nobody is perfect.*❞

❝*People will still like me if I fail from time to time.*❞

❝*Making a mistake does not mean that I fail as a person.*❞

FOCUS POINTS

● Ask yourself why you constantly need to achieve and prove yourself in order to feel good.

● Talk to others about your feelings instead of bottling them up.

ACCEPTING NEGATIVE FEELINGS

A common way of putting pressure on yourself is to deny your negative thoughts and emotions, or attempt to bury them. Avoid demanding too high a degree of virtue from yourself. Everyone has a dark side to their nature, where more negative emotions reside. Remember that feelings of anger, fear, or frustration can be healthy because they often help you to deal with pressure by spurring you on to positive action.

Coping with Demanding Routines

Stress studies show that routine irritants, such as travelling conditions, noise, pollution, and communication overload, significantly damage people's sense of well-being. With thought and planning, you can minimize these nuisances.

▲ **Using pedal power**
Cycling to work saves you money, keeps you fit, and means that you never have to be held up in traffic again. It also helps reduce stress levels by giving you time for reflective thought, and is a good way to boost your energy levels.

EASING TRAVEL PRESSURES

If your journey to work is stressful, apply creative thinking to your plight. Do you have to travel during rush hour, or could you change your time of travel? Could you negotiate working from home a couple of days a week? If you generally drive to work, are there alternative routes you could take to avoid traffic jams? Always allow plenty of time for your journey so that if there is congestion, you avoid feeling anxious. Check whether there is a station closer to your destination that you can cycle to. If your journey remains an ordeal, distract yourself by reading or learning a new skill – or think about something positive such as a forthcoming holiday.

Useful Exercises

▶ If you are stuck in traffic, do some stretches in your seat: rotate your shoulders, turn your head to stretch your neck, and stretch your arms over the steering wheel to loosen up.

▶ Make use of your journey time to think about how you would like your day to unfold.

▶ Listen to calming music if you feel anxious on a journey and uplifting music if you feel drained.

LIVING WITH NOISE AND POLLUTION

If you live in a polluted urban area or you travel to and from the city, it is important to include plenty of antioxidants in your diet by eating whole wheat and fresh fruit and vegetables such as broccoli and oranges. These contain vitamins and minerals invaluable for strengthening the immune system. Try to find a quiet place at home or at work where you can find some peace during the day – is there a local library or park within easy walking distance, for example? Viewing your home as a sanctuary can help, too. Choose a place where you feel calm – a balcony or garden, or your bedroom perhaps – and allow yourself 10 to 20 minutes of relaxation there daily. Many people find it helpful to take this time at the end of their working day to mark a change of pace.

COPING WITH COMMUNICATION OVERLOAD

It is very easy today to feel deluged by mail, and by phone, fax, and e-mail messages. Keeping a bin close to your mail collection point means that you can dump unwanted junk mail swiftly, and you can reduce the number of unwanted letters you receive by notifying junk mail companies that you do not want correspondence from them. Review subscriptions to magazines and newsletters and cancel any you are no longer interested in to save yourself time. If you want to retain any interesting pieces of reading matter for future reference, file them away immediately in one place. Both voicemail and e-mail are best dealt with by reviewing them at specific times throughout the day rather than every time you receive a message. Where possible use e-mail, since it is quicker to deal with than voice-mail.

Opens letter immediately rather than allowing mail to mount up

▲ **Opening your mail**
Try to open mail at the place where you process it and decide immediately on the priority of dealing with its contents.

Managing Major Life Changes

Pressure builds up when we struggle to cope with change. To prevent pressure from turning into stress, learn how to handle big life changes, from parenthood to bereavement.

Understanding Change

When a big change occurs, we respond, find ways of coping, and gradually resume our normal lives. This process will, inevitably, take its toll on your physical and mental welfare, so look after yourself as you prepare to move on with your life.

"Sadness flies away on the wings of time."

Jean de la Fontaine

Fact File

Experts suggest that most people take two years to recover from major life changes such as redundancy or divorce. This is the time when you come to terms with what has happened to you and assess its effects on you. Once you have experienced major changes a few times, you will become more confident about coping with new ones in the future.

LOOKING AFTER YOURSELF

When major changes happen, you may have trouble finding some stability in your life. Try to concentrate on doing one or two things well every day and avoid looking too far ahead. If you are spending a lot of time dealing with the life change, then allow yourself some time off to do something enjoyable and unrelated. Accept those bad days when you feel that you are not coping well, and congratulate yourself on the good days when you begin to feel more in control of your life. Time is a great healer, and you will eventually feel strong enough to face the future again.

Coping with the Emotions of Change

Emotion	Solution
Denial	Try to make yourself think about the change instead of ignoring it so that you gradually learn to accept it.
Numbness	Give yourself plenty of relaxation time and periods when you resolve to avoid dwelling on your changed circumstances.
Isolation	Recognize that many people do understand what you are going through and want to be able to help you.

FOCUS POINTS

● A phase of depression can be a kick-start to making positive changes in your life.

● Tell close friends and family how you are feeling when you are depressed.

RECOGNIZING DEPRESSION

If major change is making you feel isolated, you may be suffering from temporary depression. It is often necessary to go through this in order to recover from the change. Even if you are feeling unmotivated and tired, aim to do a few small tasks every day. Take note of activities that you have enjoyed and plan to do more of them. Whenever you feel depressed, write down your negative thoughts and look at them again later – they may seem less serious.

KNOWING WHEN TO MOVE ON

At a certain stage you will feel able to restart your life and move on. It is important not to rush towards this point and try to force a new beginning without having allowed yourself to go through the feelings of disruption and confusion that the cycle of change inevitably involves. Though this feeling of being in limbo may not be pleasant, it is a useful opportunity to examine – and maybe adjust – your priorities and beliefs in preparation for taking a new direction.

Rings round to find out about job opportunities

Researching your options ▶
If you are considering taking a new direction, do your homework. Gather as much information as you can before making a decision.

Adapting to Parenthood

*B*ecoming a parent and dealing with the *major life changes that come with a new baby can be a shock to many couples. To avoid a build-up of pressure, share the responsibility of caring for your baby, take rests whenever possible, and ask for help.*

FOCUS POINT

● Be patient with a partner – tiredness and mood swings affect most new parents.

SHARING RESPONSIBILITIES

Parenthood involves a huge shift in identity, and unless one parent is happy to be a full-time carer while the other earns the family income, a degree of sharing of responsibility is needed. If you are both planning to return to work, you will need to address the practicalities of combining work and parenthood. How much can you afford to spend on childcare? If you are using a nursery or childminder, who can take time off if your child is sick? Is one of you able to be home at regular times in order to schedule childcare more easily? Do you want a live-in nanny or au-pair?

◀ **Combining work and parenthood**
Balancing parenthood and work can be difficult at first, but you will soon adapt to a routine. You may even find that taking your daughter to playgroup is your favourite part of the day!

Things to Do	Things to Avoid
✔ Do join a baby group to meet parents with whom you can share concerns and swap childminding favours.	✗ Avoid becoming isolated and resentful as a result of staying at home with the baby every day and not seeing anyone.
✔ Do remember that you are your own person – take a little time each day to do something that is just for you.	✗ Avoid sacrificing your needs for those of the baby and losing your own sense of identity.
✔ Do spend time with your partner, having fun and enjoying each other.	✗ Avoid neglecting your partner and focusing all your attention on the baby.

DEALING WITH TIREDNESS

Small babies do not sleep for long periods at a time, so you need to look at ways to combat tiredness. If there are two of you and the baby is bottle-fed, you might be able to nurse the baby in shifts, with one of you doing late nights and the other doing early mornings. If the baby is breast-fed, or you are on your own, you will have to snatch opportunities to rest when the baby rests. (You may not actually sleep, but relaxing is still very beneficial.) Natural light and fresh air can ease tiredness, so try to go out at least once every day.

▼ **Accepting help**
If trusted help is available, take the chance to have a nap, or do the weekly shop, while someone else looks after your baby.

Neighbour feeds baby while mother rests upstairs

ENJOYING PARENTHOOD

For most new parents it is helpful to know people in similar situations. Ante-natal classes are good meeting places, as are parent and baby groups. Set aside time for hobbies and interests that you enjoyed before the baby was born and encourage your partner to do the same. Find a reliable babysitter and plan evenings out with your partner so that you can relax and talk undisturbed.

Case Study

NAME: Joanne
ISSUE: Feeling tired and tearful
OBJECTIVE: To seek help

Joanne is feeling irritable, tearful, and angry shortly after giving birth to her daughter. Plagued by negative feelings, she finds herself crying for no apparent reason, unable to remember anything or concentrate, and snapping at everyone. Like all new mothers, she knew to expect the "baby blues", which are due to a drop in hormone levels, fatigue, and emotional and domestic strains. She also suffers from a lack of sleep due to night feeds, but she wonders if anything else is wrong. After two weeks, she talks to her health visitor. Joanne had a complicated delivery and her health visitor reassures her by explaining that this can often cause psychological upset. Having spoken to her health visitor, Joanne feels much less guilty about her emotions and more able to deal with them. Her health visitor tells Joanne to visit her doctor if the symptoms persist.

Handling Work Changes

Pressure at work is cited as one of the biggest causes of stress today. Reduce workplace pressure by learning to manage your workload and adapt to new roles. If you are unhappy in your job, consider changing direction, or even going it alone.

> **"**Because things are the way they are, things will not stay the way they are.**"**
>
> Bertold Brecht

COPING WITH WORKLOADS

You are under pressure from work overload if you have too much work to do and not enough time to do it. If this happens, the key question to ask is "What is the purpose of this job?" Once you have clarified that, you can prioritize your tasks. Sometimes the opposite occurs, and pressure arises because of work "underload", where a job is insufficiently challenging for you. In this case, you need to ask for more variety and challenge, or consider looking for a new job.

ADAPTING TO ROLE CHANGE

In the fast-moving world of work, role change is common, and with it comes the pressure of having to adapt. Adopt a positive attitude towards change, and clarify your new role by talking to colleagues and your boss. Do not be afraid to ask for advice and information within your department. Once you feel confident in your role, set realistic standards for your progress. Remember, the most powerful learning occurs through mistakes!

Asks for advice on the hierarchy of the department

Shares knowledge of the company

Seeking advice from a colleague ▶
To clarify your role, you need to find out as much as possible, informally, about the department you are working in, and the people you are in contact with.

BECOMING SELF-EMPLOYED

If you dream of being self-employed, you need to consider what this major change involves. You must be sure that your temperament is suited to self-employment and that you will be able to cope with the different pressures that it brings. Do you have a very clear vision about what you want to do, and are you organized and self-motivated enough to do it? How will it affect your family and how will they react? If a job title and job status symbols matter to you, you may not like self-employment. Another fundamental question is, can you survive financially if things do not work out quickly?

Using your contacts
Are any of your business contacts self-employed? They may be able to give you advice on starting up on your own.

Planning a Career Change

Identify your natural abilities, experiences, and skills

⇩

Consider whether your skills lend themselves to a career that you are interested in

⇩

Find out about qualifications required, salaries, etc. in your chosen field

⇩

Research opportunities in the area you have chosen to work in

⇩

Start applying for jobs or applying to a college if you need additional qualifications

FACING UP TO REDUNDANCY

Redundancy can be a chance to make positive changes and to reappraise your direction in life. But when redundancy comes as a bolt out of the blue, you may experience feelings of denial, anger, isolation, and a sense of injustice. Work through these negative feelings before applying yourself coolly and constructively to the challenge of finding more work, perhaps in another field.

Following a dream ▶
Sometimes redundancy can be a chance for a change of direction. If you have a favourite hobby, such as gardening, could you use your talents to earn a living?

Considering Relocation

As your priorities change, you may decide to leave the pressures of your present life and relocate to somewhere that will offer you a better lifestyle. Think through your decision carefully to avoid simply swapping new pressures for old.

FOCUS POINT

● Consider and consult all family members when making any decisions about possible relocation.

Case Study

NAME: Maria
ISSUE: Stressed and exhausted
OBJECTIVE: To improve her quality of life

Combining her demanding job as a headmistress with family demands and city life is proving too stressful for Maria. After discussing their options, she and her husband, Roger, decide to relocate to the coast. Roger sells his business but continues working as a consultant. Maria and Roger move and Maria finds work within a few months. They feel that their decision has been the right one. They earn less, but spend less. They see far more of the children, and the whole family seems to be much healthier – and less stressed.

LISTING OPTIONS

Relocation involves making difficult choices based on an evaluation of your present quality of life. If you are making a move with a partner, make sure you both see the move in the same way. Will you both need to earn a living? Where relocation requires one person to become a commuter, consider whether this will simply add new pressures to your life. If you have children, are there good schools and leisure facilities nearby? Discussing all the options fully will prevent these decisions from becoming a source of stress.

Adds pros and cons to list

▲ **Planning with a partner**
Make a list together of the pros and cons of relocating. Evaluate which points are most important to each of you, and whether you both expect the same things from the move.

RESEARCHING BEFOREHAND

Make sure that your decision is the right one by going to stay in your proposed new location for a few days, or even a week. If you are thinking of moving somewhere popular with tourists, try to visit at different times of the year so that you know what life will be like both with and without the sightseers. Register with local estate agents to get an idea of what type and size of property you will be able to afford. Visit local amenities that would be important to you and your family, and try out routes and timings to the nearest town or city. Visiting local restaurants and shopping centres is a good way of finding out whether your proposed new home attracts people similar to you.

Making the Right Decision

> **Decide on your goals**

> **List all your options**

> **Research your options and think them through**

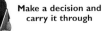

> **Make a decision and carry it through**

▲ **Getting to know a new area**
Use the time spent getting to know a new area as a time to talk to your partner and reassure yourself that you are both happy with the decision to relocate.

Moving Home

Lists of the causes of stress usually place moving home in a fairly high position. Minimize the pressures of upheaval by planning your move carefully to avoid last-minute panics, giving yourself time to settle in, and making an effort to meet new people.

FOCUS POINT

● Invite family members or close friends to visit as soon as possible so that you do not feel isolated.

Self-Talk

A period of chaos is inevitable when you move. It really helps to use assertions to encourage yourself to view the situation as temporary.

❝This chaotic period will pass quickly and then I will be settled in my new home.❞

❝I am not bothered by the mess and disruption because I have a strong sense of order surrounding the rest of my life.❞

❝I have achieved a lot by just organizing the move, so this experience has been useful.❞

PLANNING A MOVE

As soon as you are given a completion date, keep your calendar clear on the days just before and after this date, and confirm this time off at work. Then book your chosen removals company. If you can afford it – and the cost is not always prohibitive – consider paying for a complete packing and removals service. Not having to pack up all your possessions, then live with a house full of packing cases for days, or even weeks, reduces much of the pressure. The move should also be fully insured, reducing anxiety over breakages.

Rings dates on calendar to see what else needs to happen simultaneously

Reads out dates for building work and utilities to be switched over

Thinking ahead ▶
Plan ahead for your move and try to ensure that all eventualities have been envisaged, as well as coordinating your and your partner's work commitments.

- ▶ Label all the packing cases with the names of the new rooms they are destined for.

- ▶ Anticipate the financial cost of moving so that money worries do not add to the pressures of moving home.

- ▶ Check that you can get planning permission for any proposed alterations to your new house.

- ▶ Aim to get one room fit to live in straight away, so that you have a refuge to relax in at the end of the day.

SETTLING IN

Timetable your days so that you unpack and/or decorate in the mornings, and then explore the local area in the afternoons. Give yourself plenty of time to find interesting places to visit. This will boost your morale if you feel lonely or unsettled and demoralized. Loneliness and a sense of not belonging is almost inevitable when you first move somewhere new, but if you discover a walk that you really enjoy, or a restaurant that you like to visit, these small treats can make a big difference to how you feel and so will reduce the stress. Involve family members in all these activities.

Involving the entire family ▶
Young children can find moving quite stressful and unsettling. Getting them to pack and unpack their own belongings, so that they are part of the family team, may help them to feel at home in their new surroundings more quickly.

GETTING TO KNOW PEOPLE

You may find leaving old friends behind and finding new ones emotionally draining. Get to know new people by chatting to your neighbours, letting them know that you have just moved into the area. People are often very helpful about giving advice on places to visit and things to do. Explore local clubs to see if they cater to any of your interests. Be friendly to a wide circle of people at first and as you find out who you are most compatible with, you can narrow them down.

At a Glance

- ● Planning a move in detail should prevent unforeseen problems from arising.

- ● Combining unpacking with exploring will enable you to settle in to your new home.

- ● Getting to know people in your new area will stop you from feeling isolated.

Coping with Bereavement

Each person copes with bereavement in an intensely personal way, but it is vital to allow time for the grieving process. Try to reduce the immense stress caused by bereavement by accepting the need to grieve, talking to people, and looking after yourself.

> **FOCUS POINT**
>
> ● If you are having to hold a grieving family together, make sure that you do not neglect your own feelings.

Looks at photograph of friend

▲ **Sharing memories**
Using photographs and mementos to reminisce about the dead person will encourage you to talk about your feelings of loss to friends or relatives.

EXPERIENCING GRIEF

The loss of a close relative or friend always involves a period of severe grief and suffering. If the death was unexpected, there will be shock to deal with, too. If the person was very ill, there may be some relief that their suffering is over. Other feelings accompany bereavement, too: guilt about how we treated the person while alive, sadness that we never expressed our true feelings to them, or a sense of injustice about how they died. Grieving, though painful, is a natural process. It must be accepted and worked through so that pressure doesn't build up and make you ill.

Understanding the Emotions of Grief and Loss

Stage of Grief	Emotions
Shock	Feelings of denial, disbelief, incredulity, numbness, and hysteria.
Protest	Very strong feelings of anger, guilt, sadness, fear, longing, and emptiness.
Disorganization	Extremely bleak feelings of despair, fatigue, confusion, apathy, and desolation.
Reorganization	Feelings of having returned to normality but with the knowledge that life has changed since the bereavement.

SEEKING COMFORT

The less isolated you feel, the less likely it is that you will suffer from depression. Talk to friends, relatives, or counsellors who will listen and try to understand your feelings. Expressing regrets, fears, and anger is beneficial because this helps you to accept the situation. Listening to other people's experiences of and advice about bereavement can also be comforting. If you do not want to talk to relatives or friends, your doctor can recommend a counsellor. You may find talking to a stranger easier because you can say things that would be difficult discuss with someone who was also close to the deceased.

Talks about feelings of guilt, anger, and denial

▲ **Talking to a counsellor**
The benefit of talking to a counsellor is that you can explore all your emotions concerning the deceased – including any that you may feel uncomfortable about.

Useful Exercises

▶ Comfort yourself by thinking and talking about the deceased regularly. Speculate about what they would think and say about certain things.

▶ In the first months after their death, celebrate occasions that the deceased would have enjoyed to help keep their memory alive.

▶ Visit places that you used to enjoy with your loved one to remind you of the good times that you shared.

BEING KIND TO YOURSELF

It is important to accept that following the death of someone close, you may feel very tired, lose interest in work and social activities, and find yourself unable to concentrate or sleep. The grieving process has no fixed time limits, so give yourself time to adjust. Try to avoid having to make any major decisions for six months or so after a close bereavement, unless you have no choice: quite often, in order to cope with grief, we make rash decisions. Look after yourself as well as you can. Try to eat sensibly, rest often, and take light exercise. If you are not sleeping or are feeling extremely anxious or depressed, visit your doctor. Doctors can prescribe short-term medication to help people through periods of intense grief.

Dealing with Separation

W*hen a long-term relationship ends, heartache and uncertainty are unavoidable. The best way to cope with the distress of separation or divorce is to learn how to employ techniques that will help you carry on with your life.*

Case Study

NAME: Andy
ISSUE: Anger is out of control
OBJECTIVE: To move on with his life

Andy still feels angry about his divorce and is finding it hard to control his temper at work. His boss suggests that he goes to see a counsellor. Andy discusses his anger with the counsellor, who encourages him to express his feelings of anger. She also helps him devise an anger management routine so that every time he feels himself getting angry, he pauses, takes deep breaths, and does relaxation exercises. Andy feels more in control and more able to deal with his emotions concerning his marriage break-up and divorce.

COPING WITH EMOTIONS

When a major relationship ends, most people grieve in a way similar to the aftermath of bereavement. If you have instigated the separation, you may experience feelings of guilt. Instead of giving in to these feelings and perhaps returning to a bad relationship, you will need to work through the guilt. If you are the rejected partner, you may be feeling very angry. Accept that you may feel this way for a time but do not allow yourself to become bitter about what has happened.

▲ **Sharing your feelings**
Friends are very important when you are getting over the end of a long-term relationship. They can cheer you up and make you feel valued when you are grieving and your self-esteem is low.

DEALING WITH DISPLACEMENT

When a long-term relationship ends, it is not just the loss of another person's company that affects you; many other elements of life are affected, too. If you were together for a long time, you will have many shared possessions and joint friends. Your possessions need to be divided up, ideally in a calm and rational way, with compromises being made on both sides to avoid hostility. Friends may feel awkward about your split, unsure whether they can keep in touch with both of you separately, or have to choose between you. Your ex-partner's family may also be reluctant to see you after the break-up. Make it clear that you are not asking people to take sides: do your best not to drag them into your arguments.

Fact File

A recent survey revealed that 70 per cent of divorces were instigated by women. One reason for this may be that many women now have far more independence, increasing the options available to them.

Couple realize that behaviour will cause more problems than it solves

Compromise is suggested and couple part civilly

Ownership of valuable bowl becomes source of conflict

Both partners resolve to win possession

With emotions running high, couple argue bitterly and part on worst possible terms

▲ **Controlling emotion**
Separating is painful for most couples, but by keeping emotions under control and working through the problems, you can make the situation less stressful.

EASING LONELINESS

After traumatic changes such as separation and divorce, people often feel lonely. Try not to see loneliness as something to be ashamed of; see it instead as a positive emotion that is going to push you into taking steps towards leading a happy life in the future. Try to develop a positive view of single life. Focus on rediscovering who you are and building a good relationship with yourself, so that you can accept who you are and value your individuality. Give yourself small treats if you are feeling particularly low – there is nothing wrong with being self-indulgent. If you want to talk to people about your loneliness, but lack the confidence, investigate courses on self-esteem and self-confidence. Such courses build communication skills and are a great way of meeting people.

Enjoying being single ▶
There are many positive aspects to being on your own, not least of which is the freedom it gives you to do what you want to do, when you want to do it.

Fact File
Divorce or separation can result in feeling hurt, betrayed, embarrassed, or ashamed. You may feel that you can never trust anyone again. These feelings are natural. It is vital to reach out for support and caring, even if you have rarely done so in the past. Consider contacting old friends whom you have not seen for a while.

Arranges her time to suit herself

Enjoys new-found independence

Rediscovers sense of identity

Has improved social life

Indulges in favourite hobbies and pastimes

FOCUS POINTS

● Focus on the things that you had to give up for your partner and the fact that you can enjoy them now.

● Consider embarking on a new project, from clearing out the house to planning a holiday.

BEING SELF-SUFFICIENT

After a relationship ends, it is tempting to rush into another one very quickly, often out of a fear of loneliness or a desire to be loved. But it is wiser to concentrate on building a sense of self-sufficiency first, so that you know that you can survive alone, and that there are aspects of life alone that are positively enjoyable. The confidence this will give you will make you far less likely to rush into a relationship with somone who isn't right for you, but who just happens to be there at a time when you are feeling vulnerable.

MEETING NEW PEOPLE

Being in a long-term relationship can mean that you lose the knack of making new friends. Now is the time to relearn this skill, because friendship is a powerful way of reducing the pressure caused by loneliness. The best way to meet new people is through pursuing your interests. Join an evening class or take up a new sport. You are more likely to make friends with common interests in this way – whether or not any of these may offer romantic potential. Get to know people by being a good listener. Find out what their motivations and interests are by taking time to listen to them.

Self-Talk

Use the following affirmations to boost your confidence when meeting new people and to help you overcome any feelings of self-consciousness:

❝The important thing is that I'm making an effort to talk to new people.❞

❝I may be feeling shy but I can engage with others just by listening enthusiastically.❞

❝People will like me for myself.❞

❝I do have interesting things to say.❞

❝I am going to get to know this person better.❞

◀ **Broadening your horizons**
Finding a new interest increases your self-esteem and confidence. This makes it much easier to meet new friends and embark on a new relationship.

Things to Do

✓ Do take up invitations to parties to increase your chances of meeting a suitable partner.

✓ Do join a dating agency, but exercise caution when meeting new people.

✓ Do ask people out in a way that allows them to refuse without any embarrassment on either part.

Things to Avoid

✗ Avoid coming across as too aggressive or too passive due to nervousness.

✗ Avoid making excuses for not going out when the real reason is that you are nervous about meeting new people.

✗ Avoid putting yourself down so that you persuade people that you are not worth knowing.

Assessing Your Ability to Handle Pressure

*E*valuate your ability to handle pressure by responding to the following statements. Mark the answers that are closest to your experience. If your answer is "Never," mark Option 1; if it is "Always," mark Option 4; and so on. Add your scores together, and refer to the analysis to assess how well you manage when the pressure is on.

Options	
1	Never
2	Occasionally
3	Frequently
4	Always

How Do You Respond?

	1	2	3	4
1 I perform better when under pressure.	☐	☐	☐	☐
2 When I feel pressured, I understand why.	☐	☐	☐	☐
3 I know when I start to feel stressed.	☐	☐	☐	☐
4 I take steps to increase my resilience to stress.	☐	☐	☐	☐
5 I can put worries to the back of my mind.	☐	☐	☐	☐
6 I have supportive friends and family.	☐	☐	☐	☐
7 I like to ensure that I am well-organized.	☐	☐	☐	☐
8 I have time to do the things I want to do.	☐	☐	☐	☐
9 I exercise to keep myself in good shape.	☐	☐	☐	☐

	1	2	3	4
10 I am careful about what and when I eat.	☐	☐	☐	☐
11 I drink plenty of water to stay healthy.	☐	☐	☐	☐
12 I know how to unwind if I feel tense.	☐	☐	☐	☐
13 I say "no" if I do not wish to do something.	☐	☐	☐	☐
14 I express my opinions readily.	☐	☐	☐	☐
15 I stand up for myself in a disagreement.	☐	☐	☐	☐
16 I am optimistic when faced by pessimism.	☐	☐	☐	☐
17 I brush off unjust criticism.	☐	☐	☐	☐
18 If someone behaves badly, I challenge them.	☐	☐	☐	☐

		1	2	3	4
19	I do my best but I know when to stop.	☐	☐	☐	☐
20	If I make a mistake, I simply accept it.	☐	☐	☐	☐
21	My journey to work is hassle-free.	☐	☐	☐	☐
22	I have daily periods of peace and quiet.	☐	☐	☐	☐
23	I cope well when the unexpected occurs.	☐	☐	☐	☐
24	I find it easy to adapt to change.	☐	☐	☐	☐
25	If I feel sad, I know I will get over it.	☐	☐	☐	☐

		1	2	3	4
26	I enjoy my work.	☐	☐	☐	☐
27	I list options before making decisions.	☐	☐	☐	☐
28	I ask for help when I need it.	☐	☐	☐	☐
29	My hobbies help me in troubled times.	☐	☐	☐	☐
30	I am quite self-sufficient.	☐	☐	☐	☐
31	I make an effort to meet new people.	☐	☐	☐	☐
32	I am in touch with my emotions.	☐	☐	☐	☐

Analysis

When you have added up your scores, look at the analysis below to establish how well you really handle pressure. Then make a note of areas for improvement and refer to the relevant sections of the book for help.

32–64 You are at risk from stress unless you shape up mentally and physically to deal with pressure. You would benefit greatly from improving your lifestyle.

65–95 You are thriving under pressure in some areas, but need to identify those that may be causing you stress.

96–128 Your attitude and lifestyle enable you to truly thrive under pressure. Just make sure that you avoid complacency.

My weakest points are:

_____

_____

_____

_____

My strongest points are:

_____

_____

_____

Index

Acknowledgments

AUTHOR'S ACKNOWLEDGMENTS

I would like to thank Anthony Jayes and Vicki McIvor
for their contagious tenacity in this project.

PUBLISHER'S ACKNOWLEDGMENTS

Dorling Kindersley would like to thank the following for their help and participation:

Photographers Steve Gorton, Matthew Ward

Models Francesca Agati, Christine Appella, Angela Cameron, Nicolas Chinardet,
Celine Cordwell, Cynthia Gilbert, Barbara Guthrie, Deron James, Ben John, Janey Madlani,
Rosa Mignacca, Camilla Moore, Naomi Nmadu, Sagaren Pillay, Andrew Sheerin, Sheila Tait,
Suki Tan, Peter Taylor, Silvana Vieira, Jeremy Wallis.

Make-up Evelynne Stoikou

Jacket Designer John Dinsdale
Jacket Editor Jane Oliver-Jedrzejak

Indexer Hilary Bird

Picture research Anna Grapes
Picture librarian Sue Hadley

PICTURE CREDITS

Key: *a*=above; *b*=bottom; *c*=centre; *l*=left; *r*=right; *t*=top

Corbis: Darama 6*cr*, 64*br*; Rob Lewine 11*tl*; Ariel Skelley 17*br*, 61*cr*; David Raymer 24*bl*; Jeff Zaruba Studio
31*cl*; Michael A. Keller Studios, Ltd 35*br*; Tom Stewart Photography 44*br*; Mug Shots 50*cl*; Ed Bock
Photography, Inc. 54*cl*; Jack Hollingsworth 59*br*; Anthony Redpath 67*cl*; **Digital Vision Ltd:** 41*br*;
Getty Images: Ken Chernus 4; **PhotoDisc:** 23*br*, 32*bl*, 29*br*; **PhotoLink:** C. Borland 21*b*

Jacket photography © Eyewire and Dorling Kindersley

All other images © Dorling Kindersley
For further information see: www.dkimages.com

AUTHOR'S BIOGRAPHY

Philippa Davies has an MSc in psychology and runs her own business, www.getupandgrow.co.uk.
She specializes in coaching in communication and influencing skills to a wide range of eminent clients
that has included two prime ministers. Philippa wrote and presented the BBC1 TV programme *Tomorrow
the World*, about building confidence. She is also the author of several books, contributes to newspapers
and magazines, and regularly speaks at conferences on presentation skills and confidence.